ALPHABET

本書はあいうえお順レイアウトになっております。ひらがなが不得意
な方は、このＡＢＣ順のリストをご利用下さい。

AN ILLUSTRATED DICTIONARY
OF JAPANESE ONOMATOPOEIC EXPRESSIONS

AN ILLUSTRATED DICTIONARY
OF JAPANESE ONOMATOPOEIC EXPRESSIONS

英語人と日本語人のための

日本語擬態語辞典

The Japan Times

この書をすべてのパンダに捧げる

To all the pandas of the world

First edition: december 1989
14th printing: January 1999
Japanese text by OYAMA Naomi
English translation by John TURRENT
Design by Super Taco Inc.
KOBAYASHI Takashi & HIRATSUKA Masato

Published by The Japan Times, Ltd.
5-4, Shibaura 4-chome, Minato-ku, Tokyo 108-0023, Japan

ISBN4-7890-0482-1
Printed in Japan

まえがき

たとえば、歌舞伎とか文楽とか、あるいは茶道とか華道なんてものがぼくはわりあいに好きで、それなりの造詣も愛着もあるのですが、それらをひとたび「我が日本の誇るべき文化」というような視点でとらえることを好みません。むしろ嫌います。その視点で外国人に向って伝えたくもありませんし、同胞諸氏と再確認しあいたくもまたありません。まして誇らし気に説明し理解を求めたり、同意を促したりする気にもなりません。すべてそういった類のものが身近にあってね、たとえば歌舞伎にしたって、あえていえばある種の日本人が編み出した芝居のひとつの型式で、ま、それが案外洒落ていて、ぼくの好みに合うんだよね、という程度のとらえ方で、華道に造詣も愛着も深いといったところで、その本質は少しでっち上げが過ぎていて、相当屁理屈が多いねと見ているわけで、結構きびしく客観的にもとらえているわけです。けれど、ぼくのネイティブなものに対する文化観がこと「日本語における擬態語」というものに対した時にだけ、やや狂います。突然、誇らしく自慢し、説明して理解を促し、同意を得たくなります。ネイティブなものといえば、言語ほどネイティブなものはないわけですから、自らの母国語であるところの日本語そのものを誇らしく思うのが世の常なのでしょうが、何故かやはり、その気がぼくには起りません。それもまた歌舞伎と同じように、いやそれ以上に、生れた時から身近にそんなものがあってね、なんとなくぼくもそれを使って暮してきたわけで、特に誇らしくも、自慢すべきことのようにも思われません。愛着ゆえだけで誇るなら、それは

Preface

Traditional arts like kabuki, bunraku, tea ceremony, and flower arrangement give me quite a lot of pleasure, and I do have a certain degree of knowledge of and affection for them. But I do not like to consider these arts as examples of Japanese culture of which I should be proud. In fact, I very much dislike looking at them from this angle. I feel no desire at all to introduce these arts to outsiders or to share my feelings about them with other Japanese. I certainly have no wish to proudly show them off and promote understanding and approval of them.

These arts were a part of my environment when I grew up, that is all. I like kabuki simply because it is quite witty, which suits my taste. I also have some knowledge of and affection for flower arrangement, but I confess that I sometimes find this art a little too artificial and forced. You see, I look at my native culture with a very critical and objective eye.

When it comes to onomatopoeic expressions in Japanese, however, my cool attitude changes dramatically. I suddenly become very proud and boastful and have a burning desire to introduce them and get people to understand them.

Since language is the most native part of a native culture, it is no doubt normal for Japanese people to be proud of the Japanese language. For some reason, however, I do not feel such pride at all. Like kabuki, indeed even more so, the Japanese language has

よくある故郷自慢、家族自慢と同じレベルの、ただの我がままでありましょうし、やや客観的に日本語をとらえたところで、それが果して言語としてどの程度の完成度なのか、論理的にゆるぎないものなのか、はたまた、思考するための有効な手段たり得るのか、などなどという判断はつきかねます。判断すべき立場にもおりません。ですから、日本語そのものを特に外国の方々におすすめする気にはなりません。喋りたければお喋りなさい、読み書きしたくばどうぞおやり下さい、という程度。もちろん、相当むずかしいからおやめになった方が賢明ですよなどとも言いません。

しかし、「日本語における擬態語」というやつをぼくは外国人諸氏に心からおすすめします。「すきやき」も「天ぷら」もとりたててすすめないこのぼくが、「擬態語」をいちどお試しになってみたらいかがですか、という気合いでおすすめする。つまりそれがこの本なのでありますが。

それはどうやら、この「日本語における擬態語」というものの存在が、日本語の中の一つの要素、一つの品詞といったような、たとえばあまたの料理の中の天ぷら、演劇の中のひとつの型式、様式としての歌舞伎といった在り様とは根本的に違ったレベルのものだとぼくが考えているからなのです。

極端にいえば、これは本当に言葉なのかしら、とぼくは未だに迷い疑っているのです。その迷いと疑いの原因のひとつとして、品詞が決定できない、文法上、文章法上の確たる品詞として、この擬態語をとらえ切れない、ということがあります。無責任な言語学者はただ「日本語に多くの擬態

been with me since the day I was born. I grew up with it, but I do not feel any special pride in it. If affection is the only reason for being proud, then this is just the same as people boasting about their hometown or their family. It is no more than egoism.

Even if I try to look at the Japanese language objectively, I am not in a position to judge how perfect it is as a language, whether it is logically sound or whether it serves as an effective vehicle for thoughts. So I have no special desire to recommend the Japanese language itself to foreigners. If they want to speak it, fine. If they want to read and write it, that is fine too. Of course, I am not going to advise people to give up because it is too difficult, either.

But while I do not especially recommend foreigners to try kabuki, or sukiyaki, or tempura, I have no hesitation in recommending them to try Japanese onomatopoeic expressions. This is why I set about compiling this book. Kabuki is one form of Japanese drama, and tempura is one type of Japanese cuisine, but onomatopoeic expressions are much more than just one part of the Japanese language.

I often wonder whether onomatopoeic expressions are really words, because grammatically they cannot be defined as any specific part of speech. Lazy linguists usually skip over the topic by saying something like "the Japanese language has a large number of onomatopoeic expressions." And more diligent linguists only touch on them

語あり」で済ませていますし、少し賢い学者はこの言葉群が表面的にもつ幼稚性、非論理性等を理由に、あまり深く言及いたしません。つまり本気には扱わないのです。扱えないといった方が正しいでしょう。それも無理はないな、とぼくは考えます。これは、とても専門家の言語学者が分化した学問として扱えるような代物ではないのです。だって、そもそもこれは言語ではないんですから。敢えていえば「言語の素」みたいなものなのです。言語のカオス、カオス状態の言語、それこそ、もやもや、どろどろ、ごちゃごちゃ、ばらばら、ふわふわ、などと擬態語そのものをもってしか表現し得ないような、さて、これから必要とあらば言語にでもなりましょうか、とゆったりとくくっているような状態の言葉群なのですから、かしこい、ただしい、えらい、あるいは立派な、というような、ゆるぎない形容詞、形容動詞等をもって表現し得るような人々にはなかなか扱えません。下手に扱うとエライ目にあいます。ぼくぐらいが扱うのが丁度いいのです。なにしろぼくは、もやもや、どろどろ、ごちゃごちゃ、そして、ぐだぐだ、へらへら、うろうろ、の専門家ですからね。そしてさらに、けっして日本語の専門家たり得ない、つまり日本語をネイティブ・ランゲージにしていない人々こそ、この言葉群を扱える有資格者です。そしてたとえば、動物学者が、観察し、捕獲し、研究し、分類し、と懸命にアプローチしたところで、当の動物はほとんどそれには無頓着に勝手に生きているのと同じように、言葉も学問的な管理にはほとんどなじまず、それこそ生き物そのものでありますから、勝手気ままに生きてゆくわけであります。それが動物、それが言葉、

briefly, because, they say, onomatopoeic expressions are childish and illogical.

So linguists do not deal with onomatopoeic expressions. Or perhaps I should say, they are unable to deal with them. And this is not surprising; onomatopoeic expressions are not the kind of subject matter that expert linguists can take up as a separate topic and study academically. After all, onomatopoeic expressions are not really language; they are, in a sense, raw language. *Moya moya, doro doro, gocha gocha, bara-bara, fuwa fuwa* — no other words can describe these expressions. They represent a world of their own — a group of expressions on the verge of becoming words if necessary. Linguists, who are always described by such orthodox adjectives as *kashikoi* (wise), *tadashii* (right), *erai* (great), or *rippana* (respected), cannot handle them. If they handle them carelessly, they will run into problems.

Onomatopoeic expressions are just right for a person like myself, because I am a specialist when it comes to being *moya moya, doro doro*, and *gocha gocha*, not to mention *guda guda, hera hera*, and *uro uro*. You do not have to be an expert in the Japanese language to appreciate these expressions; indeed, non-native speakers are probably even more qualified to handle them than Japanese linguists. In the same way as animals go on living quite indifferently while zoologists zestfully observe, capture, study, and classify them, words go on living despite the efforts of schol-

そんな、ま当り前のことを改めて思い起させてくれるような力がこの「日本語における擬態語」というものには確実にあります。ですから、この言葉の世界を楽しく味わっていただけたら、日本語そのものの理解というよりはむしろ、言葉とは何かというような、やや壮大なテーマが案外気楽に考察できるのではないかと思います。それになにはともあれ、これは日本語には違いないのであり、さらに「日本語の素」なのですから、このままでもすぐにお使いになれますし、ちょっと手を加えていただけたら、立派な一品にもなるはずです。ぼくはすきやき、天ぷらより、「擬態語」をおすすめします。お試し下さい。

五味太郎

ars to manage them. Onomatopoeic expressions remind us of this natural state of affairs.

If you enjoy the world of onomatopoeic expressions, I think they will help you understand something about not so much the Japanese language itself as the somewhat grander topic of the nature of words. And of course, these expressions are part of the Japanese language; indeed, they are raw Japanese, so you will be able to use them as they are. And if you add a little more, you will be speaking wonderful Japanese. I do not necessarily recommend sukiyaki or tempura, but I do suggest you try these onomatopoeic expressions. I am sure you will relish them.

GOMI TARO

凡 例

❶ 日本語において「擬態語・擬音語」と呼ばれるものにはさまざまな形がある（〈例〉せっせ あんぐり からから くしゃくしゃ あたふた ちょこまか こけこっこう）が、ここでは「いじいじ」「あっぷあっぷ」のように同じ音の組み合わせを二度繰り返す、いわゆる「重ねことば」と呼ばれるものに限って取りあげた。

また、文法的には副詞として扱われているもの（〈例〉いよいよ わざわざ）、動詞や形容詞を重ねたもの（〈例〉のびのび あつあつ）など、本来、擬態語・擬音語には分類されていないものもあえて取りあげた。

❷ 擬態語・擬音語には個人的な感覚によるも

Introduction

❶ Japanese has several types of onomatopoeic expressions that describe sounds or actions; for example, *sesse, anguri, karakara, kushakusha, atafuta, chokomaka, kokekokkō*. This dictionary covers only those expressions that are formed by repeating the same sound twice, such as *ijiiji* and *appuappu*. In Japanese such words are called *kasanekotoba* (repeated words).

I have also included in this dictionary some common repeated words that are not usually classified as onomatopoeic expressions, such as *iyoiyo* and *wazawaza*, which are used as adverbs, and *nobinobi* and *atsuatsu*, which are formed from verbs or adjectives.

の、方言特有のもの、古語や流行語などさまざまあるが、ここでは現代共通語として用いられていると思われるものを取りあげた。

❸ 見出し語と語源が同じ、あるいは何らかの因果関係があると思われる言葉（〈例〉うきうき―浮く しずしず―静かだ）については、意味の最後に☆印をつけて記した。

❹ 本書では見出し語を文法上、大きく以下の3つに分類した。

[A]：副詞タイプ

活用がなく、おもに連用修飾語として用いるもの。以下の3種類がこれに含まれる。

（i）一般的に副詞と呼ばれているもの
末尾に「と」を伴わないで、そのままの形で用いる。
〈例〉いよいよ出発だ　いちいちうるさい
　　　わざわざ届ける

（ii）そのまま、あるいは末尾に「と」を伴って、副詞として用いるもの
〈例〉おずおず（と）差し出す
　　　ほかほか（と）温かい

（iii）末尾に「と」を伴って、副詞として用いるもの
〈例〉ろうろうと歌う　もんもんと悩む

[B]：サ変動詞タイプ

末尾に動詞「する」を伴って、サ行変格活用型の複合動詞として用いるか、あるいは格助詞「と」＋「する」を伴って用いるもの
〈例〉うきうき（と）して　ぼさぼさ（と）した髪
　　　うじうじするな

[C]：形容動詞タイプ

末尾に形容動詞の活用語尾を伴って用いる。ただし、後ろに名詞がくる場合（連体形）には、

❷ There are many kinds of onomatopoeic expressions. Some derive from individual tastes, some belong to local dialects, some have become archaic, and some are in fashion for only a short time. This dictionary deals only with words that are widely used in standard Japanese today.

❸ Words that have the same root as the onomatopoeic expression or some other close connection with it, such as *uku* for *uki uki* and *shizukada* for *shizushizu*, are included after a ☆ mark following the explanation.

❹ In this dictionary, onomatopoeic expressions are classified into three grammatical types.

[A]: Adverbial type

Used mainly as modifiers for verbs or adjectives. There are three types:

(i) Expressions that are classified as adverbs and used as adverbs as they are, without any particle.

Examples: *iyo iyo shuppatsu da*
　　　　　(nearly time to leave)
　　　　　ich ichi urusai
　　　　　(always complaining)
　　　　　waza waza todokeru
　　　　　(going out of your way to deliver something)

(ii) Expressions used as adverbs either as they are or with the particle *to*.

Examples: *ozu ozu (to) sashidasu*
　　　　　(to hold out nervously)
　　　　　hoka hoka (to) atatakai
　　　　　(glowing with warmth)

(iii) Expressions used as adverbs with the particle *to*.

Examples: *rō rō to utau*
　　　　　(to sing loudly and clearly)

形容動詞の活用語尾「―な」の代わりに、「―の」を用いる場合が多い。おそらく、「―の」は「―な」の音便形だと思われる。

〈例〉意見がばらばらだ　へとへとに疲れる
　　　あつあつの二人（＝あつあつな二人）

❺ 見出し語の意味が2つ以上あり、意味によって文法上の分類が異なる場合には、意味の番号と品詞の番号を一致させた。

〈例〉かんかん ① 激怒する様子（彼はかんかんだ）…………………… ①[C]
　　　　　　② 太陽が強く照りつけるさま（日がかんかん照る）……… ②[A]

❻ 本文中ではアクセントについては触れていないが、一般的に[A]タイプ、[B]タイプは第1アクセント、[C]タイプのものは第1音が低く、第2音以降が高いアクセントで発音するものが多い。
なお前項で述べたように、一つの見出し語でも意味によって形容動詞に属したり副詞に属したりするものがあり、この場合、当然アクセントも異なってくるから要注意。

〈例〉つ｜るつる(と)すべる　つ｜るつるした表面
頭がつ｜るつるだ

❼ ここで取りあげた言葉の中には、❹で分類した3つの用法以外に、名詞的な用法をもつものもある（〈例〉いらいらが募る　顔にぶつぶつができた　文句たらたら　いよいよの時　彼はまだまだだ）が、本書ではこれらを[A][B][C]と別の用法として分類してはいない。
なぜなら、これらは元をただせば「いらいら(とした感情)が募る」「顔にぶつぶつ(したもの)ができた」といった具合に、被修飾語が省略され

mon mon to nayamu
(to worry despairingly)

[B]: Compound verb type
Used as verbs with *suru* or with the particle *to* and *suru*.
Examples: *uki uki (to) shite*
(buoyantly)
bosa bosa (to) shita kami
(unkempt hair)
uji uji-suru na
(Don't be bashful.)

[C]: *Na* adjectival type
Used with an inflection of the *na*-type adjective. When the expression is followed by a noun, *no* is often used instead of the inflection *na*.
Examples: *iku ga bara bara da*
(opinions were divided)
heto heto ni tsukareru
(to be worn out)
atsu atsu no futari
(a couple in love)

❺ When the onomatopoeic expression has two or more meanings, the number of the part of speech corresponds to the number of the meaning.
Example:
kan kan ① Describes someone who is very angry·················· ①[C]
② Describes the burning sun or burning coal················· ②[A]

❻ This dictionary does not touch on pronunciation, but in general the high pitch accent falls on the first syllable of an onomatopoeic expression in the case of [A] and [B] types and on the second and following syllables in the case of [C] type, with the first syllable being pronounced in a low pitch.
Examples: *tsu｜ru tsuru (to) suberu*

たもの、すなわち[A]タイプや[B]タイプが変形
したものにすぎないからである。

❽❹の文法上の分類は、現代の常識的な用
法の一端を示したにすぎない。したがって、今日
「てくてく(と)歩く」のようにもっぱら副詞的に用い
ているものでも、近い将来「てくてくする」と言いな
らされる可能性は大いにあるし、現在、❼のよう
な名詞的な用法がないとされているものでも「お
なかのしくしくが治まらない」という具合に流動的
に用いることに何の制約も不備もない。むしろ、
ここでの分類にとらわれない自由な使い方をする
のが、擬態語の本来の姿であるから、その可能
性、流動性を十分含んだうえで、この辞書を
ご活用いただきたい。

tsu｜ru tsuru-shita hyōmen
atama ga tsu｜ru tsuru da

❼ Besides the three grammatical categories mentioned above, some onomatopoeic expressions can be used as
nouns. For example:

ira ira ga tsunoru (Irritation builds
up.)
kao ni butsu butsu ga dekita (A rash
appeared on his face.)
monku tara tara (endless complaining)
iyo iyo no toki (the final stage)
kare wa mada mada da (He still has
some way to go.)

This book does not give this usage a
separate classification, because in fact
the nouns are only shortened forms of
[A] or [B] types. In the above examples, *ira ira* is short for *ira ira to shita
kanjō* and *butsu butsu* for *butsu butsu-
shita mono*.

❽ The grammatical categories mentioned above are nothing more than
guidelines based on common usage
today. It is quite possible that in the
near future an onomatopoeic expression
now used as an adverb (for example,
teku teku to aruku) will be used as a
compound verb (*teku teku-suru*), and
more onomatopoeic expressions will be
used as nouns (*onaka no shiku shiku ga
osamaranai*). It is this flexibility that
gives onomatopoeic expressions their
true character. Please bear this in mind
when you refer to this dictionary.

本文見出し語の後の括弧内のA、B、C、は凡例❹の文法上の分類を示すA.副詞タイプ、B.サ変動詞タイプ、C.形容動詞タイプのそれぞれの略号である。各見出し語についての用法は略号に従って凡例を参照されたい。

Each onomatopoeic expression in this book is followed in parentheses by one or more of the letters A, B, or C. These letters refer to the grammatical classification of onomatopoeic expressions explained in paragraph ❹ of the Introduction, with A standing for adverbial type, B for compound verb type, and C for adjectival type. For an explanation of usage, please refer to the Introduction.

3

atsu atsu [c]

Describes something that looks piping hot.
Also used to describe a couple who are head
over heels in love. ☆*atsui*

あつあつ

見るからに熱い様子。男女の仲がと
てもよい様子にも用いる。☆熱い

appu appu [A][B][C]

Describes someone floundering in water and almost drowning. Also used to describe someone in trouble or difficulty. In deep water.

あっぷあっぷ

おぼれかけて、もがいているさま。とても困って苦しんでいる様子にも用いる。

iki iki [A][B]

いきいき

Describes someone or something that is full of life. Lifelike. Vivid. ☆*ikiru*

元気、活気がある様子。生きがいい
さま。☆生きる

iji iji [A][B]

Describes someone unable to be honest or frank in front of others. Also describes reserved, timid, or servile behavior or attitude. Cowardly. ☆ *ijikeru*

いじいじ

素直に人に対することができず、行動や態度がはっきりしないさま。卑屈な様子。☆いじける

iso iso [A] [B]

Describes someone who moves as if full of joy
or expectation. Cheerfully. Excitedly.

いそいそ

喜びや期待で、動作が調子づく様
子。

1

ichi ichi [A]

One by one. In detail. Persistently. ☆*ichi*

いちいち

ひとつひとつ。子細もらさず。しつこく。
☆一（いち）

iya iya [A]

Reluctantly. With a heavy heart. ☆*iyada*

いやいや

いやだが、しかたなく。☆いやだ

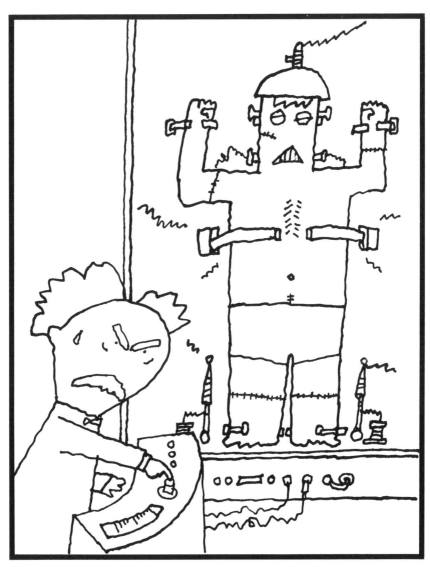

iyo iyo [A]

①At last. ②Even more. ③Without doubt; decidedly. ④The final stage of something.

いよいよ

①ついに。②今までよりいっそう。③確かに。決定的に。④極限の状態。

ira ira [A] [B]

Describes someone who is irritated or angry because things are not going as desired.

いらいら

思いどおりにならないため、あせって落ち着かず、腹立たしいさま。

uki uki [A][B]

Describes someone who is happy and excited.
In a buoyant mood. ☆*uku*

うきうき

うれしくて、心がはずむ様子。浮かれ
るさま。☆浮く

uji uji [A][B]

Hesitant, irresolute. Used to describe someone who wants to do something but cannot bring himself or herself to do it.

うじうじ

態度がはっきりしない様子。何かをしたいと思いながら決断がつかずにいるさま。

uja uja [A]

Describes many small things gathered together and moving, such as a swarm of insects or a crowd of people seen from a distance.

うじゃうじゃ

小さな虫などがたくさん集まってうごめいているさま。

UZU UZU [A][B]

Describes someone itching to do something.
☆ *uzuku*

うずうず

何かがしたくてたまらず、落ち着かない様子。☆うずく

uda uda ①[A][B] ②[A]

① Describes someone who is slow and lazy.
Idle. ② Describes someone saying something
meaningless in a drawn-out manner.

うだうだ

①てきぱき行動せず、怠惰に過ごす
様子。②無意味なことをくどく言うさま。

uto uto [A][B]

Describes someone dozing. Napping.

うとうと

いねむりしている様子。もっぱら眠る形
容に用いる。

uro uro [A][B]

Describes someone wandering about aimlessly
or someone who has lost sight of their goal.
Loafing around. Hanging around.

うろうろ

あてもなく、または目的を見失って、あ
たりをさまよう様子。

OZU OZU [A]

Describes behaving in a fearful or diffident manner. Gingerly. ☆ *ozu (ojiru)*

おずおず

おそれながら、あるいは遠慮がちに
行動する様子。☆おず(おじる)

ota ota [B]

Describes someone who is too surprised or shocked to respond properly.

おたおた

驚きあわてて、まともに何もできないでいる様子。

odo odo [B]

Describes someone who is restless with fear
or uncertainty. Cowering.

おどおど

恐れや不安で落ち着かない様子。

1

oro oro [B]

Describes someone who is confused and does not know what to do. Flustered.

おろおろ

どうしていいかわからず、とり乱すさま。

3

gakugaku ①[A][B][C] ②[A][B]

① Describes something that was fixed in place but comes loose and begins moving, such as a loose tooth. ② Describes part of the body trembling.

がくがく

①固定してあったものがゆるんで動く様子。②体の一部が小刻みにふるえるさま。

kachi kachi ①[A] ②[C]

① Describes the sound made when solid objects hit each other. ② Describes something very hard. Also used to describe someone's strait-laced views or to describe a person who is stiff with nervous tension. Rigid.

かちかち

①硬いものがぶつかり合う音。②とても堅いさま。人の考え方が堅苦しい様子や、緊張などで体が硬くなっている様子にも用いられる。

gatsu gatsu [A] [B]

Describes someone eating greedily. Also used
to describe someone who hungers after something. Crave.

がつがつ

むさぼり食うさま。何かを貪欲に求め
る様子にも用いる。

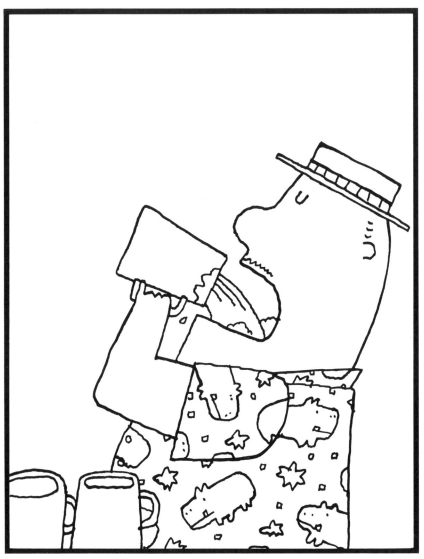

gabugabu [A]

Describes someone downing a large drink thirstily. Gulping down. Guzzling.

がぶがぶ

大量の液体を勢いよく飲む様子。

gami gami [A]

Describes someone nagging. Griping.

がみがみ

口やかましく文句を言うさま。

gayagaya [A][B]

Describes a noisy situation, with many people speaking at the same time. Hubbub.

がやがや

大勢の話し声が響いて騒がしい様子。

kankan ①[C] ②③[A]

①Describes someone who is very angry. In a rage. ②Describes the burning sun or burning coal. ③Describes the clanging sound made when metal or other hard objects hit each other.

かんかん

①激怒する様子。②太陽が強く照りつけるさま。炭がさかんに燃えているさま。③金属など硬いものがぶつかって出る、高く澄んだ音。

gisu gisu [B]

① Describes a relationship or an atmosphere that lacks friendliness. Strained. ② Describes someone who is thin and bony.

ぎすぎす

①親しみやゆとりがないさま。②やせて骨ばった様子。

kibi kibi [A][B]

Describes attitude, behavior, or speech that is prompt, businesslike, and alert.

きびきび

態度・言動が敏速で無駄がなく、小気味よい様子。

gyū gyū ①[A] ②[A][C]

①Describes the sound of crinkling leather or a creaking door. ②Describes pushing, packing, or closing something as strongly or tightly as possible. ③Describes bringing someone to their knees by severely reproaching or drilling them.

ぎゅうぎゅう

①物がこすれたり、きしんだりして出る鈍い音。革製品がこすれる音など。②余裕がなくなるほど強く力を加えるさま。押す、詰める、締めるなどの形容に用いる。③強く責めたり鍛えたりして、参らせる様子。

43

kyoro kyoro [A][B]
Describes someone looking around restlessly.
Staring about.

きょろきょろ

落ち着きなく、あたりを見回すさま。

gira gira [A][B]

Describes something shining brightly. Dazzlingly. Also used to describe a person's appearance or look. Glaring.

ぎらぎら

強く輝く様子。どぎつく光るさま。態度、視線などにも用いる。

gui gui [A]

Describes doing something forcefully and continuously, such as gulping down a drink or pulling someone by the hand.

ぐいぐい

力強く、連続して何かをおこなう様子。飲む、引っ張る、進むなどの形容に用いる。

kusa kusa [B]

Describes someone who is feeling depressed
because something unpleasant has happened.
Feeling blue. ☆ *kusaru*

くさくさ

いやなことがあって、気分が晴れない
さま。☆腐る

GUZUGUZU ①②[B]③[A]④[C]

① Describes sluggish, dillydallying behavior. ② Describes something that is uncertain, such as the weather. ③ Describes someone who is grumbling or complaining. ④ Describes something that has lost its shape. Loose. ☆*guzuda*

ぐずぐず

①行動が敏速でないさま。②(天気など)様子がはっきりしないさま。③不平を言うさま。④形がくずれて、しまりがないさま。☆ぐずだ

kuta kuta [C]

Describes something that is withered. Also used to describe someone who is very tired. Worn out. Exhausted.

くたくた

張りがなく、しおれた様子。とても疲れた様子にも用いる。

gucha gucha ①②[A][B][C]③[A]

① Describes something soft and soggy. Also describes the action of stirring or mashing such a substance. ② Describes something in awful disarray. Higgledy-piggledy. ③ Describes grumbling.

ぐちゃぐちゃ

①水分をたっぷり含んで柔かい様子。または、水分を含んだものをかき回したりつぶしたりする様子。②ひどく乱れた様子。③ぐちっぽく、あれこれ言う様子。

kudo kudo [A]

Describes saying the same thing over and over again. Tediously. ☆*kudoi*

くどくど

同じことをしつこく繰り返して言うさま。
☆くどい

kunekune [A][B]

Describes something that curves gently several times. Meandering. Also used to describe someone wriggling his or her body. ☆*kuneru*

くねくね

何度もゆるやかに曲がるさま。また、体をよじるさまにも用いる。☆くねる

kuyo kuyo [A][B]

Describes worrying for ages about a trivial matter. Moping. Brooding.

くよくよ

ささいなことをいつまでも気に病む
様子。

kura kura [A][B]
Describes having a dizzy spell. Feeling giddy.

くらくら

目まいがして、倒れそうな様子。

kurukuru [A]

① Describes a small object spinning lightly.
② Describes quickly winding up a long object, such as string. ③ Describes someone who is quick at moving or coming up with ideas.
④ Describes a situation in which changes are kaleidoscopic.

くるくる

①連続して軽快に回転する様子。②長いものを手早く幾重にも巻きつけるさま。③動作や頭の回転が早くて活発な様子。④変化がめまぐるしいさま。

guru guru [A]

① Describes something spinning round and round. ② Describes winding something round and round or rolling something up. ③ Describes moving something again and again.

ぐるぐる

①連続して回転する様子。②幾重にも巻きつけるさま。③次々に移動させる様子。

gungun [A]

Describes something progressing or growing very rapidly.

ぐんぐん

力強く、進み方がめざましいさま。

kechi kechi [A][B]

Describes someone who is stingy with money
or other things. Tightfisted. ☆ *kechida*

けちけち

お金や品物をいかにも惜しそうにする
さま。☆けちだ

keba keba [A][B]

Describes someone or something that is gaudy.
Garish. ☆*kebakebashii*

けばけば

派手でどぎついさま。☆けばけばしい

gera gera [A]

Describes laughing in a noisy, uncontrolled manner. Guffawing loudly.

げらげら

大声で、しまりなく笑うさま。もっぱら笑う形容に用いる。

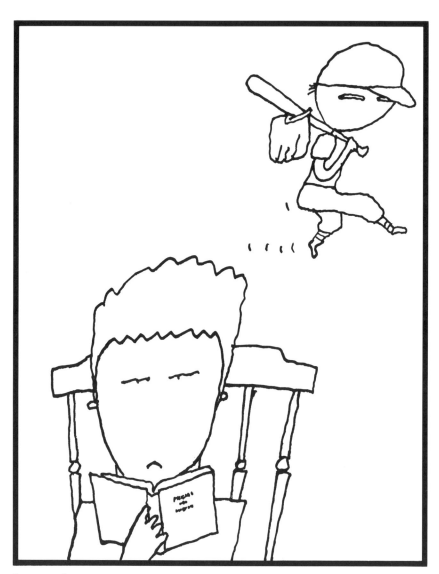

koso koso [A][B]

Describes stealthy movement to avoid being discovered by others. Like a thief in the night.

こそこそ

人に知られないように、ひそかに行う
様子。

goso goso [A][B]

Describes a jarring sound or something that makes such a sound. The sound of rummaging.

ごそごそ

耳ざわりな音がするさま。また、そういう音を立てて動き回るさま。

gocha gocha ①[A][B][C] ②[A]

① Describes a jumble. ② Describes someone
complaining about one thing and another.

ごちゃごちゃ

①多くの物が入り乱れて、雑然とし
た様子。②あれこれ不平不満を言
い立てるさま。

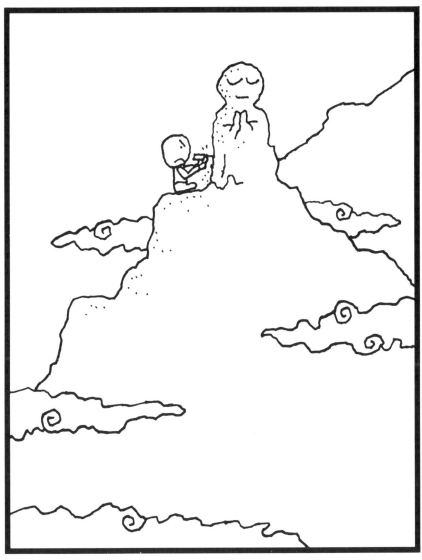

kotsu kotsu [A]

① Describes the sound of a hard object hitting something, such as shoes hitting the pavement or someone knocking at a door. Tapping. Clicking. Drumming. ② Describes someone grinding away at their job. Unflaggingly.

こつこつ

①硬いものが打ち当たって発する音。舗道を歩く靴音、ノックの音など。②地道な努力を続けるさま。

koro koro ①②④[A] ③[A][B][C]

① Describes something small and round rolling over. ② Describes a high, clear, pleasant sound, such as the ringing of a bell or a young girl's giggle. ③ Describes something fat and round. ④ Describes something, such as the topic of conversation, that changes frequently.

ころころ

①小さく丸いものがころがるさま。②高く澄んで、響きのよい音。鈴の音、若い女性の笑い声などの形容に用いる。③太って、いかにも丸いさま。④ある状態に、たやすく何度も至る様子。話が変わる形容などに用いる。

kowagowa [A]

Describes nervous, frightened behavior. With trepidation. ☆*kowai*

こわごわ

こわがりながら行うさま。☆こわい

gowa gowa [B][C]

Describes something that has become stiff, such as paper or cloth.

ごわごわ

紙、布などが固くこわばった様子。

zā zā [A]

①Describes the sound of rushing water. Often used to describe the sound of pouring rain. ② Describes the sound of static on television or loudspeakers.

ざあざあ

①水が勢いよく流れる音。特に、雨が激しく降る音の形容によく用いる。② テレビ、スピーカーなどの雑音。

zaku zaku [A][B]

①Describes a large number of metal coins or jewels. ②Describes the sound of chopping vegetables or the like. Also describes cutting something roughly. ③Describes the sound of gravel or the like being mixed. ④Describes the sound of walking over gravel or frost.

ざくざく

①金貨、宝石などがたくさんある様子。②野菜などを切り刻む音。また、切り方が粗いさま。③粗い粒状のものが混ざり合う音。④砂利や霜柱などを踏んで歩く音。

saba saba [B]

① Describes the feeling of relief one has after settling an irritating or unpleasant matter. Getting a load off one's mind. ②Describes someone who is plain-spoken. Candid. ☆*sabaku*

さばさば

①面倒なことや嫌なことが片づいて、すっきりした様子。②性格がさっぱりしているさま。☆さばく

samu zamu [B]

Describes a cold, bleak scene. Wintry. Desolate.
☆ *samui*

さむざむ

いかにも寒そうなさま。殺風景な様子。
☆寒い

same zame [A]

Describes someone crying bitterly. Broken-heartedly. Sorrowfully.

さめざめ

涙を流し、しのび泣くさま。もっぱら、
泣く形容に用いる。

shikushiku ①[A] ②[A][B]

① Describes someone weeping. Sobbing. ②
Describes a dull pain. Often used to describe
stomachache or toothache.

しくしく

①静かに泣き続けるさま。②鈍い痛
みが続くさま。腹痛や歯痛の形容に
用いる。

shige shige [A]

①Describes taking a close look. Scrutinize.
Ogle. ②Describes visiting a place frequently.

しげしげ

①よく観察する様子。②頻繁に通う
さま。

shizu shizu [A]

Describes someone acting or moving quietly.
Gracefully. ☆*shizukada*

しずしず

静かに行動するさま。しとやかな様子。
☆静かだ

jito jito [A][B][C]

Describes an unpleasantly hot and damp atmosphere. Sweaty.

じとじと

湿気や水分が多く、不快なさま。汗
ばむ様子。

shibushibu [A]

Describes doing something reluctantly. Grudgingly. ☆*shibui*

しぶしぶ

やむを得ず。気が進まないが、しかたなく。☆渋い

shimijimi ①[A][B] ②[A]

① Describes feeling something keenly. ②
Describes doing something quietly. Calmly.
☆*shimiru*

しみじみ

①身にしみて感じるさま。②心静か
に、落ち着いておこなう様子。　☆染
みる

shā shā [A][B]

Describes someone remaining unmoved despite having done something deserving reproach. Brazen-facedly. Shamelessly.

しゃあしゃあ

非難されるべきことをしながら、平気でいる様子。あつかましいさま。

jabujabu [A]

Describes the sound and action of splashing water.

じゃぶじゃぶ

水をかき回すときに出る音。また、その
様子。

jirijiri [A][B]

①Describes someone running out of patience and fretting. ②Describes something that draws closer little by little. ③Describes the scorching sun. ④Describes something that has been burned. ⑤Describes the sound of an alarm bell.

じりじり

①待ち切れず、じれる様子。②少しずつ、迫るように進む様子。③直射日光が照りつけるさま。④焼け焦げるさま。⑤ベルなどが鳴る音。

jirojiro [A]

Describes someone staring rudely.

じろじろ

無遠慮に見つめるさま。もっぱら、見る
形容に用いる。

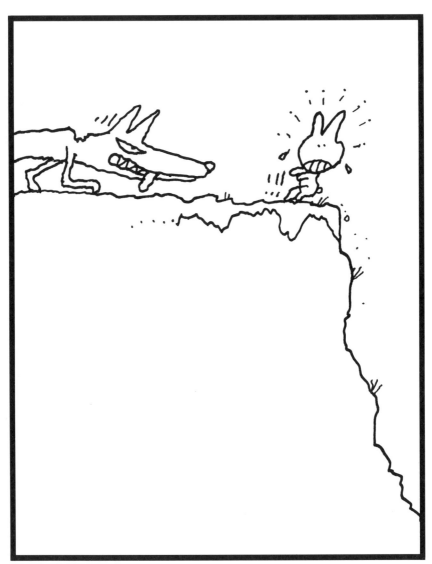

jiwajiwa [A]

Describes something advancing slowly but
steadily.

じわじわ

物事が、ゆっくりではあるが確実に進
んでいく様子。

sui sui [A]

Describes moving smoothly and easily through something, such as someone swimming gracefully or a car moving swiftly along an empty street.

すいすい

水中、空中などを軽やかに進む様子。乗り物などが滞りなく進むさま。

zuka zuka [A]

Describes someone making an entrance boldly
or rudely.

ずかずか

無遠慮に入り込むさま。もっぱら、入り
込む、踏み込むなどの形容に用いる。

zuki zuki [A][B]

Describes a throbbing pain, including heart-break.

ずきずき

傷が脈打つように、絶えず強く痛むさ
ま。心の痛みにも用いる。

sukusuku [A]

Describes growing healthily and steadily.

すくすく

すこやかに、順調に伸び育つ様子。

zuke zuke [A]

Describes speaking bluntly. Brusquely.

ずけずけ

無遠慮に、はっきりとものを言う様子。

sugo sugo [A]

Describes leaving a place in low spirits. De-
jectedly.

すごすご

気落ちして、元気なくその場を立ち去
るさま。もっぱら立ち去る、帰るなど、そ
の場から離れる形容に用いる。

zuta zuta [c]

Describes something torn. Ragged. Also used
to describe a deeply broken heart.

ずたずた

細かく切れたり裂けたりしたさま。心
が深く傷ついた形容にも用いる。

suya suya [A]

Describes sleeping peacefully. Soundly.

すやすや

やすらかに眠っている様子。もっぱら、
眠る形容に用いる。

sura sura [A]

Describes something proceeding smoothly. Without a hitch. Often used to describe eloquent speech or writing.

すらすら

動作または物事が、よどみなく順調に進むさま。話す、書くなどの形容によく用いる。

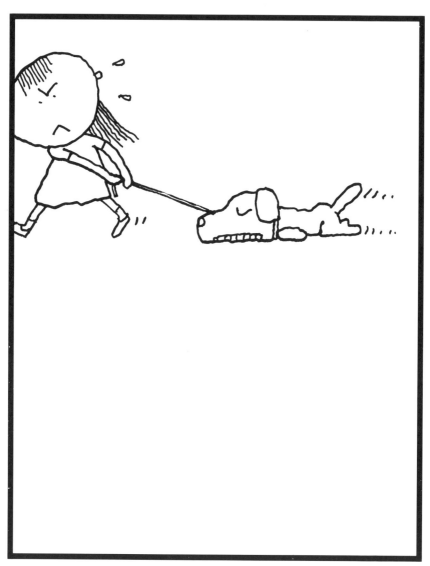

zuruzuru ①[A] ②③[A][C]

① Describes the sound or act of dragging. Also describes the sound made by someone slurping food. ② Describes something that is loose. ③ Describes an undesirable situation that drags on inconclusively.

ずるずる

①物を引きずったり、すすったりする音や様子。また、引きずられるように滑り落ちるさま。②しまりがないさま。③けじめがつかず、望ましくない状態が長びく様子。

sure sure [c]

Describes being extremely close. Also used to describe something that has almost reached or exceeded the limit. On the verge of.

すれすれ

非常に接近しているさま。また、もう少しで限度を越えそうな様子にも用いる。

sekaseka [A][B]

Describes someone who acts impetuously. Hastily. ☆*sekasu*

せかせか

動作や態度が落ち着かず、気ぜわしいさま。☆せかす

zoku zoku [A][B]

① Describes a feeling of chilliness. ② Describes someone who is so tense or excited that their body trembles or a chill runs down their spine. Expresses fear, anticipation, joy, or emotion. ※A homonym of this word describes something continuing without interruption.

ぞくぞく

①寒けを感じるさま。②体が震えたり背筋に寒けを感じたりするほど、緊張したり興奮したりするさま。恐怖、期待、喜び、感動などを表す。※べつに、途切れることなく続くさまを表す同音異義語「ぞくぞく（続々）」あり。

sorosoro [A]

① Describes doing something slowly and quietly. ② Describes a situation or time that is approaching. On the brink of.

そろそろ

①ゆっくり、静かにおこなうさま。②ある状態や時期になりかかった様子。まもなく。

zoro zoro [A]

①Describes a large number of people or things standing in line. ②Describes trailing a skirt or the like in a slovenly way.

ぞろぞろ

① 人や物がたくさん並んで続く様子。②着物の裾などを、だらしなく引きずるさま。

sowasowa [A][B]

Describes someone who is nervously excited
about something.

そわそわ

何かに気を取られて、落ち着かない
さま。

taji taji [A]

Describes someone retreating, overwhelmed by
the power of another. Recoiling. Flinching.
Cringing. ☆*tajirogu*

たじたじ

相手の力や勢いに圧倒されて、あと
ずさりする様子。ひるむさま。☆たじろぐ

dabu dabu [B][C]

Describes clothing that is too big. Loose.
Baggy.

だぶだぶ

衣服などが大きすぎて、体に合わない
さま。

tara tara [A]

①Describes water or any other liquid that is dripping. ②Describes endless complaining or boasting.

たらたら

①液体がしたたり落ちるさま。②文句、自慢など、いい加減にやめてほしいことを際限なく言う様子。

dara dara ①③[A] ②[A][B]

①Describes water or any other liquid that is streaming. ② Describes something that goes on for a long time without conclusion. Also describes dilatory behavior. Dillydallying. ③ Describes a long, gentle slope.

だらだら

①液体が流れ出るさま。②長々と続いて、しまりがない様子。また、動作が緩慢なさま。③ゆるやかな傾斜が続くさま。

chikuchiku [A][B]

Describes a sharp object pricking something
and also the pain felt from such a prick.

ちくちく

先のとがったもので、小刻みに刺す
様子。また、そのような痛みを感じる
さま。

chibi chibi [B]

Describes doing something little by little to
make it last as long as possible. For example,
sipping a drink. ☆ *chibiru*

ちびちび

もったいなさそうに、ちょっとずつ。
☆ちびる

chokochoko ①②[A][B] ③[A]

①Describes walking or running with short steps. Toddling. Hobbling. ②Describes someone who is restless and constantly on the move. ③Describes getting something done easily without much time or effort.

ちょこちょこ

①小股で早歩きしたり走ったりするさま。②落ち着かず、たえず動き回っている様子。③時間や手間をかけず、物事を簡単に済ませる様子。

chira chira [A][B]

① Describes something small and light drifting down. Fluttering. ②Describes a light that flickers or appears to flicker. ③ Describes something that is seen or heard intermittently. Also used to describe someone casting glances at something.

ちらちら

①小さく軽いものがひるがえりながら落ちるさま。②光が小刻みに明滅するさま。また、そのように感じるさま。③断続して見えたり聞こえたりする様子。視線を何度かすばやく走らせるさまにも用いる。

tsuka tsuka [A]

Describes heading straight for a destination without any hesitation. Walking briskly. Marching.

つかつか

ためらわずに進み出るさま。もっぱら、歩み寄るなど、目的に向かっていく形容に用いる。

tsuya tsuya [A] [B]

Describes a shining surface. Glossy. Glistening.
Sheeny. ☆tsuya

つやつや

表面に光沢があって美しいさま。
☆つや

tsuru tsuru ①[A][B][C] ②[A]

①Describes a smooth surface. Polished. Also describes slipping on a smooth surface. ②Describes the sound made by someone slurping noodles.

つるつる

①表面がなめらかなさま。また、なめらかなものに触れてすべるさま。②麺類をすするさま。

tsun tsun ①③[A][B] ②[A]

①Describes someone being prim and unsociable. Aloof. Describes someone being sullen ,and morose. ② Describes something pointed, or something pointed that is growing. ③ Describes a sharp smell.

つんつん

①とりすまして取っつきにくいさま。機嫌が悪く無愛想な様子。②先がとがった様子。また、とがったものが伸びるさま。③刺激的な臭いが鼻をつくさま。

tekuteku [A]

Describes walking quite a distance at a steady pace.

てくてく

かなりの距離を地道に歩き続ける様子。もっぱら歩く形容に用いる。

dere dere [B]

Describes a loose attitude or appearance. Often used to describe a man's spoony attitude toward a woman.

でれでれ

態度、身なりなどにしまりがない様子。特に、男が女に対してだらしない態度をとる形容に多く用いる。

113

dokidoki [A][B]

Describes a pounding heart. Palpitating. Beating fast.

どきどき

心臓が激しく鼓動する音や様子。

tobo tobo [A]

Describes walking wearily. Trudging.

とぼとぼ

元気なく歩く様子。もっぱら、歩く形容に用いる。

doro doro ①[C] ②[A][B][C] ③[B]

① Describes something covered in mud. ② Describes a liquid that is opaque and sticky. Syrupy. ③ Describes mixed emotions. Muddled. ☆ *doro*

どろどろ

①泥がたくさんついたさま。②液体が不透明で粘りけが強いさま。③感情などが複雑に絡んで、すっきりしない状態。☆泥

tonton [A]

①Describes the sound of gentle knocking or of someone going up or down the stairs. Tapping. Clip-clop. ② Describes something going well. ③ Describes two things that are just about the same. Equal. Often used to describe equal gain and loss.

とんとん

①軽く打ち当たる音が連続するさま。ノックや階段を上り下りする音など。②物事が順調に運ぶ様子。③二つのものがだいたい同じで差がない様子。特に、損得が同じ形容によく用いる。

dondon [A]

① Describes a continuous loud sound like the beating of a drum or someone stamping their feet on the floor. ② Describes something that proceeds steadily or someone going ahead with something without hesitation.

どんどん

①力強く打ち当たる音が連続するさま。太鼓の音、床を踏みならす音など。②物事が滞ることなく進むさま。また、物事をためらわずに進めるさま。

nā nā [c]

Describes carrying something out through collusion or compromise.

なあなあ

なれあい、妥協で済ませること。また、その様子。

naganaga [A]

Describes something that is prolonged. Drawn-out. Lengthy. Often used to describe a speech that goes on longer than necessary. ☆ *nagai*

ながなが

いかにも長いさま。話などが、必要以上に長たらしい様子。☆長い

nayo nayo [A][B]

Describes someone or something that is weak.
Delicate. Supple.

なよなよ

しなやかで弱々しいさま。

niko niko [A] [B]
Describes someone smiling happily. All smiles.

にこにこ
うれしそうにほほえむさま。

niya niya [A][B]

Describes smiling in a faint, meaningful manner.
Grinning.

にやにや

意味ありげに薄笑いする様子。

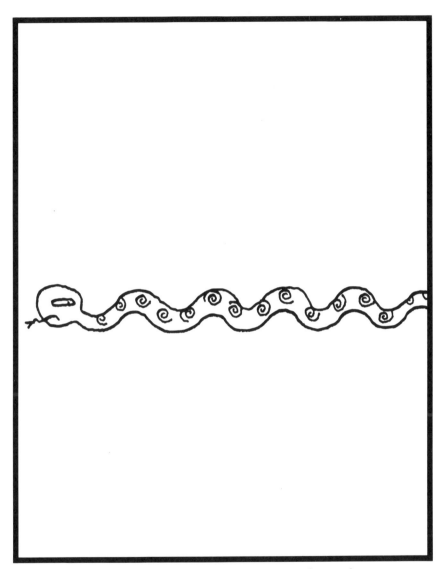

123

nyoro nyoro [A][B]

Describes something long and thin, like a snake,
moving along with a wriggling motion.

にょろにょろ

細長いものが身をくねらせて進むさま。

nukunuku [A]

①Describes having a feeling of warmth and comfort. Snugly. Cosily. ②Describes someone having an easy, carefree time.

ぬくぬく

①暖かく心地よいさま。②何の苦労もせず、いい思いをしている様子。

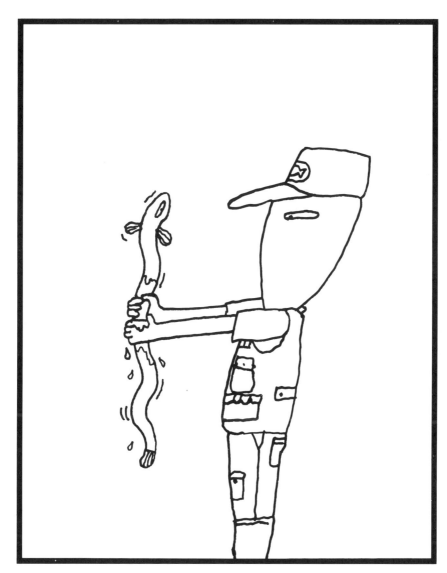

nurunuru [A][B]

Describes something slimy and slippery.

ぬるぬる

表面にぬめりがあって滑りやすいさま。
また、そのもの。

nechi nechi [A][B]

①Describes something sticky. Gluey. ②Describes tenacious character, behavior, or speech. Persistent.

ねちねち

①しつこく粘りつくさま。②性格や言動がしつこいさま。

neba neba [A][B]

Describes something that is sticky and clings easily. ☆ *nebaru*

ねばねば

粘りけがあって他のものにくっつきやすいさま。また、そのもの。☆ねばる

noko noko [A]

Describes someone appearing at a place quite nonchalantly, when he or she should really feel ashamed. Shamelessly. Casually. Unknowingly.

のこのこ

来ては具合が悪いはずの場に、平気で、あるいは何も知らずに出てくる様子。

noso noso [A][B]

Describes moving slowly, clumsily. Often used to describe the movement of large people and animals. Lumbering.

のそのそ

動きが鈍いさま。体が大きい人や動物の動きを表すことが多い。

nobinobi [A][B]

Describes doing something in an easy and re-laxed manner. Describes someone relaxing without any interruptions or worries. Leisurely. Expansive. ☆*nobiru* ※A homonym of this word describes something postponed many times. Put off again and again.

のびのび

自由でゆったりとしたさま。邪魔なものや心配事がなく、くつろいだ様子。
☆伸びる ※べつに、何度も延期される様子を表す同音異義語「のびのび（延び延び）」あり。

noro noro [A][B]
Describes moving slowly. Sluggishly. ☆ *noroi*

のろのろ
動きがおそく、鈍いさま。☆のろい

haki haki [A][B]

Describes speaking clearly or behaving with
alacrity. Lucidly.

はきはき

言葉や態度が明確で歯切れよい
さま。

pakupaku [A][B]

Describes someone opening and closing their mouth many times. Often used to describe someone eating heartily or a flap that keeps opening and closing.

ぱくぱく

口を大きく何度も開閉するさま。食べ方が盛んな様子や、物の合わせ目が開いたり閉じたりする様子などに用いる。

bata bata ①③[A][B] ②[A]

① Describes the sound of a flag or banner flapping in the wind. Fluttering. Also describes making a sound by shaking such objects. ② Describes objects falling down in succession. Also describes things taking place in rapid succession. ③ Describes someone in a rush.

ばたばた

①布や板状のものが風にはためいたり打ち当たったりする音。また、それらを小刻みに動かして音を立てるさま。②物が次々に倒れるさま。また、物事が立て続けに行われる様子。③あわただしくふるまう様子。

hara hara [A][B]

①Describes being anxious about how things are going to turn out. Apprehensive. ②Describes petals or tears falling gently. Trickling down.

はらはら

①事のなりゆきを心配して、気づかう様子。②花びら、涙などが少しずつ静かに落ちるさま。

bara bara ①[A] ②[A][C] ③[C]

① Describes the sound of hailstones or acorns falling to the ground. ② Describes things scattered about or something that constituted a whole but has broken up. In bits and pieces. ③ Describes something that lacks unity. Disjointed. In disorder.

ばらばら

①粒状のものが続けざまに落ちる音や様子。②散在するさま。また、一つにまとまっていたものが離れ離れになる様子。③物事に統一がない様子。

bari bari ①②[A] ③[C]

① Describes the act or the sound of tearing, chewing, or crunching something. ② Describes an energetic action. ③ Describes something hard and stiff.

ばりばり

①厚みがあるものを力強く裂いたり噛んだり引っかいたりする音や様子。②物事を精力的にこなすさま。また、その人。③物が堅くこわばっているさま。

138

pika pika [A][B][C]

Describes something sparkling. Glittering. Shining. Also used to describe something that is brand new.

ぴかぴか

光り輝くさま。また、ま新しい様子を比喩的にいうこともある。

hikuhiku [A][B]

Describes light convulsions in part of the body. Twitching.

ひくひく

体の一部などがかすかにけいれんする様子。

bikubiku [A][B]

①Describes part of the body shaking gently. Trembling. ②Describes someone who is afraid or nervous. Scared.

びくびく

①体の一部などが小刻みに震え動く様子。②恐怖や不安におびえるさま。

bisho bisho [c]

Describes someone or something that is sopping wet. Soaking. Wet through.

びしょびしょ

雨や水にひどく濡れたさま。

hiso hiso [A]

Describes talking so that others cannot hear.
Whispering. Speaking in a hushed voice.
☆ *hisokada*

ひそひそ

他人に聞かれないように、小声で話
す様子。☆ひそかだ

hiya hiya [B]

ひやひや

Describes being very frightened because of danger or uncertainty. Scared half to death. Terrified. ☆*hiyasu*

危険や不安を感じて、気が気でない様子。☆冷やす

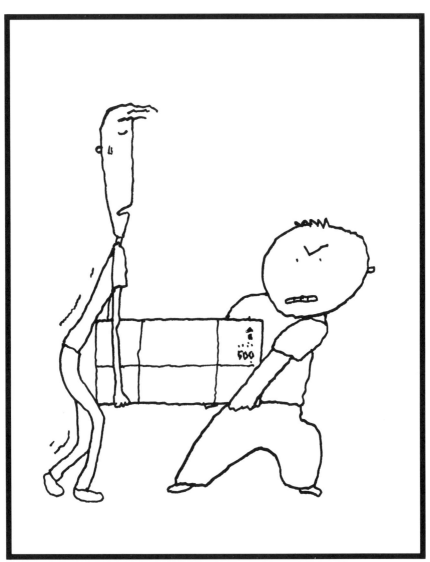

hyoro hyoro [A][B][C]

Describes someone or something long and frail. Lanky. Also describes someone unsteady on their feet. Shaky. Swaying.

ひょろひょろ

細長く伸びて、か弱そうなさま。また、力なく足元がおぼつかない様子。

145

pyon pyon [A]
Describes hopping or skipping agilely.

ぴょんぴょん
繰り返し、身軽にはねるさま。もっぱら
飛ぶ、はねるなどの形容に用いる。

hira hira [A][B]

Describes objects like paper, a handkerchief, or petals falling. Fluttering. Swirling. Also used to describe a butterfly flying.

ひらひら

紙、布、花びらなど、薄くて軽いものがひるがえって揺れたり散ったりする様子。蝶が飛ぶ形容にも用いる。

hiri hiri [A][B]

Describes stinging pain. Also used to describe a burning mouth after eating hot food.

ひりひり

皮膚に痛みなどの刺激を感じるさま。辛さが口の中を刺激するさまにも用いる。

biri biri ①③[A][B] ②[A][C]

①Describes the feeling one gets from an electric shock or the like. ②Describes the sound or act of tearing something up forcefully. Ripping. ③Describes the sound of something vibrating, such as a glass window rattled by a strong wind.

びりびり

①電気ショックなどで体がしびれる様子。また、そのような刺激を感じるさま。②紙、布などを勢いよく引き裂く音や様子。③物が小刻みに振動して出す音。また、その音が響くさま。爆風を受けたガラス窓の音など。

bukubuku ①[A][B][C] ②[A]

① Describes something outrageously fat. Flabby. Obese. ② Describes the sound or act of bubbles or foam rising or of something giving off bubbles while sinking. Also used to describe the sound of gargling.

ぶくぶく

①しまりなく太ったさま。②泡立つ音や様子。泡を出しながら沈んでいくさま、うがいをするさまにも用いる。

butsu butsu ①②④[A] ③[A][B]

① Describes muttering in a small voice. ②
Describes complaining. Grumbling. ③ Describes something with many small holes or
lumps. Rash. ④ Describes continuously pierc-
ing or cutting something into small pieces.

ぶつぶつ

①小声でつぶやくさま。②不平を言
うさま。③小さな穴や突起がたくさん
あるさま。また、そのもの。④何度も突
き刺したり、短く切ったりするさま。

bura bura [A][B]

① Describes a rather heavy object that is dangling and swaying. ② Describes walking without any real purpose or walking slowly. Strolling. ③ Describes spending time without any proper job or schedule. Loafing around. Drifting through life.

ぶらぶら

①やや重いものが垂れ下がって揺れ動く様子。②さしたる目的もなく歩くさま。また、ゆっくり歩くさま。③決まった仕事や日課がなく、漫然と過ごすさま。

buru buru [A][B]

Describes something shaking. Trembling. Also used to describe someone's body shaking from cold or fear. Shivering. Quaking.

ぶるぶる

小刻みに振動するさま。また、寒さや恐怖で体が震えるさま。

pun pun ①[A][B][C] ②[A][B]

①Describes someone who is very angry. ②Describes a strong smell hanging over a place.

ぷんぷん

①ひどく怒っているさま。怒りちらすさま。②強いにおいがたちこめる様子。

peko peko ①②[A][B] ③[C]

① Describes the sound or act of a thin sheet of metal or plastic being bent back and forth. Twanging. ②Describes bowing humbly many 'times and assuming a servile attitude. ③ Describes being very hungry. Famished. Ravenous.

ぺこぺこ

①薄い金属板などがへこんだり戻ったりする音や様子。②何度も頭を下げるさま。何かにつけて下手に出て、こびへつらうさま。③ひどく空腹なさま。

beta beta ①③[A][B][C] ②[A][B]

①Describes something sticky or clingy. ②Describes someone clinging to anothers. Often used to describe a man and woman who stick closely together. ③Describes covering a surface with paint, pieces of paper, or signatures.

べたべた

①粘りつくさま。②まとわりつくさま。特に、男女がやたらにくっつきあう形容によく用いる。③一面をおおうように、塗りつけたり、いくつも紙を貼ったり判を押したりする様子。

heto heto [c]

Describes being so tired that one has no strength left. Exhausted. Pooped out.

へとへと

体じゅうの力が抜けるほど、ひどく疲れ
切った様子。

hena hena [A][B][C]

① Describes curving or bending. ② Describes someone becoming weak through loss of mental or physical strength. Buckling under. Ready to drop.

へなへな

①曲がったりしなったりするさま。②気力や体力がなくなったり弱まったりするさま。

hera hera [A][B]

Describes laughing frivolously or ambiguously. Also used to describe frivolous speech and behavior.

へらへら

意味もなく軽薄に笑うさま。あいまいに
笑うさま。また、言動が軽々しい様子。

bera bera [A]

Describes speaking endlessly. Wagging one's tongue. Especially used to describe someone who goes so far as to say something they should not.

べらべら

とめどなくしゃべりまくるさま。特に、言うべきではないことまでしゃべる様子によく用いる。

pera pera ①③[A] ②[A][C] ④[B][C]

① Describes chattering away frivolously. Glibly. ② Describes speaking fluently in a foreign language. ③ Describes leafing through a book. Thumbing through. ④ Describes cloth or wooden boards that are thin and cheap-looking.

ぺらぺら

①軽薄によくしゃべるさま。②外国語を流暢に話すさま。③紙などを続けてめくるさま。④布、板などが薄くて安っぽいさま。

pero pero [A]

Describes putting the tongue out and moving it around. Licking.

ぺろぺろ

舌を出して、盛んに動かすさま。舌で
なめ回すさま。

hoka hoka [A][B][C]

Describes something warm, especially warm, delicious-looking food. Steaming hot.

ほかほか

温かいさま。特に、食べ物が湯気が立つほど温かくておいしそうな形容によく用いる。

pokapoka ①[A][B][C] ②[A]

① Describes a feeling of warmth throughout one's body. ② Describes the sound or act of beating someone. Thumping.

ぽかぽか

①体の中まで暖かく気持ちいい様子。②続けざまに殴る音や様子。

bosa bosa [A][B][C]

Describes unkempt, ruffled hair. Also used to describe the ragged tip of a broom or paintbrush.

ぼさぼさ

髪が乱れているさま。箒や筆などの毛先が不揃いな様子にも用いる。

pota pota [A]
Describes dripping water.

ぽたぽた

液体がしたたり落ちるさま。

hoyahoya [C]

Describes something new or fresh, such as a newly wed couple or a new employee.

ほやほや

できたて、生まれたての状態。また、ある状態になって間もないさま。新婚や新入社員の形容などによく用いる。

boro boro ①[C] ②[A][B][C] ③[A]

① Describes something badly damaged. Also describes being mentally and physically worn out. ② Describes falling grains. Also describes something that has lost its cohesion and crumbled. ③ Describes wrongdoings or lies that are uncovered one after another.

ぼろぼろ

①物がひどく傷んだ様子。また、心身が疲れ切ったさま。②粒状のものが次々にこぼれ落ちるさま。また、水分や粘りがなくなって、粒々が離れ離れになった様子。③悪事やうそなどが次々に露見するさま。

majimaji [A]

Describes taking a long, hard look at something. Staring.

まじまじ

じっと見つめるさま。視線をそらさず見据えるさま。もっぱら見る形容に用いる。

mada mada [A]

①Describes still having some way to go before reaching the goal. Short of the mark. ②Describes more of something to come, such as more reasons or more food. ☆ *mada*

まだまだ

①ある状態・程度・段階に達するにはほど遠いさま。②同じような事柄がその他にもたくさんあるさま。☆まだ

machimachi [C]

Describes things that are different. Diverse. Often used to describe things that could easily be the same but actually differ from one another. Varied.

まちまち

それぞれ異なる様子。同じでよいと思われるものが、一つ一つ違う場合に用いることが多い。

mie mie [C]

Describes seeing through another person's scheme, especially lies or flattery. ☆ *mieru*

みえみえ

相手の意図、特にウソやお世辞など
が見えすいているさま。☆見える

mukamuka [A][B]

① Describes feeling sick. Queasy. ② Describes a surge of anger.

むかむか

①吐き気がするさま。②怒りがこみあげてくるさま。

mushi mushi [A][B]

Describes hot, humid weather. Muggy. ☆ *musu*

むしむし

湿度が高く、暑いさま。☆蒸す

muzumuzu [A][B]

① Describes an itchy feeling. Ticklish. ② Describes being impatient at not being able to do something one wants to do.

むずむず

①虫がはうようなかゆみを感じるさま。②何かをしたいのにできなくて、落ち着かない様子。はがゆいさま。

175

munya munya [A]
Describes muttering something meaningless.
Often used to describe sleep talking.

むにゃむにゃ
わけのわからないことを口の中でつ
ぶやく様子。また、寝言をいうさま。もっ
ぱら、言う形容に用いる。

munmun [A][B]

Describes a stuffy or crowded atmosphere. Also used to describe a woman's or group of women's amorousness.

むんむん

熱気や人いきれがいっぱいに充満している様子。女の色気が立ちこめるさまにも用いる。

mekimeki [A]

Describes progressing or growing rapidly and
visibly. Conspicuously.

めきめき

進歩、成長などが目立って早いさま。

meso meso [A][B]

Describes uncontrolled weeping. Sobbing. Also describes an effeminate man crying endlessly.

めそめそ

弱々しく泣くさま。すぐ涙ぐんだり、い つまでも泣いたりして女々しい様子。 もっぱら、泣く形容に用いる。

mojimoji [A][B]

Describes someone behaving nervously or bashfully and unable to do what they want to do. Hesitantly.

もじもじ

遠慮したり恥ずかしがったりして、したいことができずにためらっているさま。

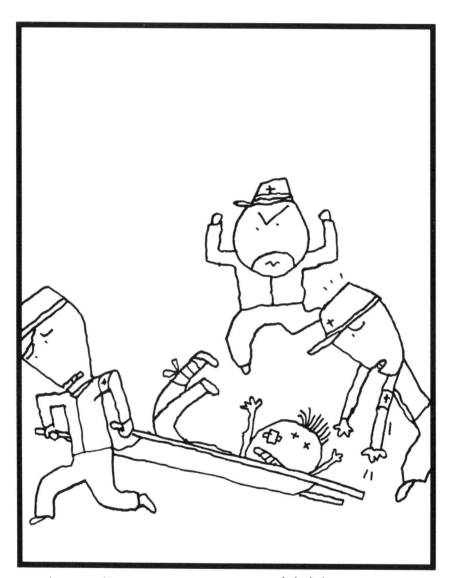

mota mota [A][B]

Describes behavior or actions that are slow
and inefficient. Clumsy.

もたもた

動作や物事の進行がのろくて、要領
を得ない様子。

morimori ①[A][B] ②[A]

① Describes something that rises powerfully. Swells.　② Describes someone full of zest or someone acting zestfully. Full of gusto. ☆ *moru*

もりもり

①力強く盛り上がるさま。②意欲、元気などがさかんにわきおこるさま。また、意欲的、精力的に物事をおこなう様子。☆盛る

monmon [A][B]

Describes someone worrying about something
for a long time but unable to find a solution.
In anguish. ※Always followed by *to*.

もんもん

ひどく悩み苦しむさま。深く思い悩ん
でも解決の糸口が見つからず、長時
間苦しみ続ける様子。※つねに末尾に
「と」を伴って用いる。

183

yasuyasu [A]

Describes doing something with ease. Without
difficulty. Effortlessly. ☆*yasui*

やすやす

いかにも簡単そうに。たやすく。☆や
すい

yū yū [A]

Describes behaving confidently. Calmly. With plenty of leeway.

ゆうゆう

あわてず落ち着いているさま。十分余裕があるさま。

yusa yusa [A]

Describes the swaying of something large and heavy, such as a tree. ☆ *yusaburu*

ゆさゆさ

大きなもの、重いものがゆっくり大きく
ゆれる様子。もっぱら、ゆれる、ゆする
などの形容に用いる。☆ゆさぶる

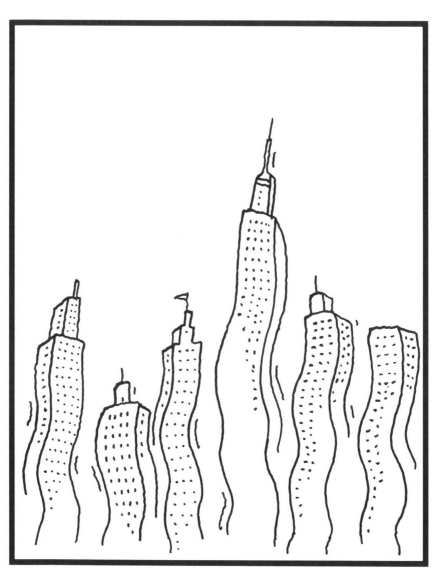

yura yura [A][B]

Describes slow swaying. Swinging. Rolling. Wobbling.

ゆらゆら

ゆるやかにゆれ動くさま。もっぱら、ゆれる形容に用いる。

yuruyuru ①[B][C] ②[A]

① Describes something very loose. ② Describes slow movement. ☆ *yurui*

ゆるゆる

①とてもゆるいさま。ゆるんださま。②急がずゆっくり動くさま。☆ゆるい

yobo yobo [A][B][C]

Describes something weak and unsteady from old age.

よぼよぼ

年老いて、見るからに体力がなかったり足元がおぼつかなかったりする様子。

189

yoro yoro [A][B]

Describes something unsteady on its feet and
unstable. Tottering.

よろよろ

足取りが乱れて、体が不安定なさま。

rōrō [A]

Describes singing or reciting in a loud, clear voice. ※Always followed by *to*.

ろうろう

声が大きく、澄みわたったさま。もっぱら、歌う、吟ずるなどの形容に用いる。
※つねに末尾に「と」を伴う。

wai wai [A]

Describes a large number of people behaving
boisterously. Making a din.

わいわい

大勢が大声で騒ぐさま。

wakuwaku [A][B]

Describes someone who is bursting with ex-
citement in anticipation of something. Thrilled.

わくわく

期待やうれしさで、胸がおどる様子。

193

waza waza [A]

① Describes doing something on purpose, even though there is no need to. ② Describes doing something specially rather than incidentally. ☆ *wazato*

わざわざ

①そうする必然性がないのに、故意にするさま。②何かのついでではなく、そのためだけにするさま。特別に。
☆わざと

wanwan [A]

① Describes a dog's bark. Bowwow.* ② A child's word for a dog. *Incidentally, a cat mews *nyā nyā*, a cow moos *mō mō*, a pig oinks *bū bū*, a goat bleats *mē mē*, a crow caws *kā kā*, a sparrow tweets *chun chun*, and a frog croaks *kero kero*, and a fish goes.....?

わんわん

①犬の鳴き声*。②幼児語で、犬そのもの。 *ちなみに、ねこは「にゃあにゃあ」、牛は「もうもう」、ぶたは「ぶうぶう」、やぎは「めえめえ」、からすは「かあかあ」、すずめは「ちゅんちゅん」、かえるは「けろけろ」、さかなは…?

おもな重ねことば一覧

A List of Common Japanese Repeated Words

●印はこの本で紹介したもの

Expressions marked with a dot (●) are explained
in this dictionary.

あおあお	ao ao	●うじうじ	uji uji
あかあか	aka aka	●うじゃうじゃ	uja uja
あきあき	aki aki	うすうす	usu usu
●あつあつ	atsu atsu	●うずうず	uzu uzu
●あっぷあっぷ	appu appu	●うだうだ	uda uda
あとあと	ato ato	うちうち	uchi uchi
あへあへ	ahe ahe	うつうつ	utsu utsu
あらあら	ara ara	うつらうつら	utsura utsura
ありあり	ari ari	●うとうと	uto uto
あれあれ	are are		
		うねうね	une une
		うはうは	uha uha
いがいが	iga iga	うようよ	uyo uyo
●いきいき	iki iki	うらうら	ura ura
●いじいじ	iji iji	●うろうろ	uro uro
●いそいそ	iso iso	うんうん	un un
●いちいち	ichi ichi		
いちゃいちゃ	icha icha	えっさえっさ	essa essa
●いやいや	iya iya	えんえん	en en
●いよいよ	iyo iyo		
●いらいら	ira ira	おいおい	oi oi
いろいろ	iro iro	おさおさ	osa osa
		●おずおず	ozu ozu
うかうか	uka uka	おせおせ	ose ose
●うきうき	uki uki	おそるおそる	osoru osoru

195

●おたおた	ota ota	●がぶがぶ	gabu gabu
おちおち	ochi ochi	がぼがぼ	gabo gabo
●おどおど	odo odo	●がみがみ	gami gami
おのおの	ono ono	●がやがや	gaya gaya
おめおめ	ome ome	からから	kara kara
おもいおもい	omoi omoi	がらがら	gara gara
おやおや	oya oya	からんからん	karan karan
おりおり	ori ori	かりかり	kari kari
●おろおろ	oro oro	がりがり	gari gari
おんおん	on on	かるがる	karu garu
		かわるがわる	kawaru gawaru
●がくがく	gaku gaku	●かんかん	kan kan
かさかさ	kasa kasa	がんがん	gan gan
がさがさ	gasa gasa		
かしゃかしゃ	kasha kasha	きいきい	kii kii
がしゃがしゃ	gasha gasha	ぎいぎい	gii gii
かすかす	kasu kasu	ぎこぎこ	giko giko
かずかず	kazu kazu	ぎざぎざ	giza giza
かたかた	kata kata	きしきし	kishi kishi
がたがた	gata gata	ぎしぎし	gishi gishi
がたんがたん	gatan gatan	●ぎすぎす	gisu gisu
●かちかち	kachi kachi	きちきち	kichi kichi
がちがち	gachi gachi	ぎちぎち	gichi gichi
かちゃかちゃ	kacha kacha	きちんきちん	kichin kichin
がちゃがちゃ	gacha gacha	きつきつ	kitsu kitsu
かちんかちん	kachin kachin	ぎとぎと	gito gito
かつかつ	katsu katsu	●きびきび	kibi kibi
●がつがつ	gatsu gatsu	きゃあきゃあ	kyā kyā
がっぱがっぱ	gappo gappo	ぎゃあぎゃあ	gyā gyā
かねがね	kane gane	きゃっきゃっ	kyak kya(k)
がばがば	gaba gaba	きゃぴきゃぴ	kyapi kyapi

196

●ぎゅうぎゅう	gyūgyū	くっくっ	kukku(k)
きゅっきゅっ	kyukkyu(k)	ぐつぐつ	gutsugutsu
きょときょと	kyotokyoto	ぐでんぐでん	gudenguden
●きょろきょろ	kyorokyoro	●くどくど	kudokudo
ぎょろぎょろ	gyorogyoro	くにゃくにゃ	kunyakunya
きらきら	kirakira	ぐにゃぐにゃ	gunyagunya
●ぎらぎら	giragira	●くねくね	kunekune
きりきり	kirikiri	ぐびぐび	gubigubi
ぎりぎり	girigiri	●くよくよ	kuyokuyo
ぎろぎろ	girogiro	●くらくら	kurakura
ぎんぎん	gingin	ぐらぐら	guragura
		くりくり	kurikuri
●ぐいぐい	guigui	ぐりぐり	guriguri
くうくう	kūkū	●くるくる	kurukuru
ぐうぐう	gūgū	●ぐるぐる	guruguru
●くさくさ	kusakusa	くるんくるん	kurunkurun
ぐさぐさ	gusagusa	ぐるんぐるん	gurungurun
くしゃくしゃ	kushakusha	くろぐろ	kuroguro
ぐしゃぐしゃ	gushagusha	くんくん	kunkun
ぐしょぐしょ	gushogusho	●ぐんぐん	gungun
くすくす	kusukusu		
●ぐずぐず	guzuguzu	げこげこ	gekogeko
●くたくた	kutakuta	げじげじ	gejigeji
くだくだ	kudakuda	げそげそ	gesogeso
ぐたぐた	gutaguta	けたけた	ketaketa
ぐだぐだ	gudaguda	げたげた	getageta
ぐちぐち	guchiguchi	●けちけち	kechikechi
くちゃくちゃ	kuchakucha	けちょんけちょん	kechonkechon
●ぐちゃぐちゃ	guchagucha	●けばけば	kebakeba
ぐちゅぐちゅ	guchuguchu	けらけら	kerakera
ぐちょぐちょ	guchogucho	●げらげら	geragera

197

けろけろ	kero kero	ごみごみ	gomi gomi
げろげろ	gero gero	こもごも	komo gomo
		こらこら	kora kora
こうこう	kō kō	こりこり	kori kori
ごうごう	gō gō	こりごり	kori gori
ごきごき	goki goki	ごりごり	gori gori
ごくごく	goku goku	●ころころ	koro koro
ごしごし	goshi goshi	ごろごろ	goro goro
こせこせ	kose kose	ころんころん	koron koron
●こそこそ	koso koso	ごろんごろん	goron goron
●ごそごそ	goso goso	●こわごわ	kowa gowa
ごたごた	gota gota	こんこん	kon kon
こちこち	kochi kochi	ごんごん	gon gon
●ごちゃごちゃ	gocha gocha	●ごわごわ	gowa gowa
こちょこちょ	kocho kocho		
ごちょごちょ	gocho gocho	さあさあ	sā sā
こっくりこっくり	kokkuri kokkuri	●ざあざあ	zā zā
●こつこつ	kotsu kotsu	さくさく	saku saku
ごつごつ	gotsu gotsu	●ざくざく	zaku zaku
ごつんごつん	gotsun gotsun	ざっくざっく	zakku zakku
ごてごて	gote gote	ざっくりざっくり	zakkuri zakkuri
こてんこてん	koten koten	ざっざっ	zaz za(z)
ことこと	koto koto	さてさて	sate sate
ごとごと	goto goto	●さばさば	saba saba
ごとんごとん	goton goton	ざぶざぶ	zabu zabu
こなごな	kona gona	ざぶんざぶん	zabun zabun
ごにょごにょ	gonyo gonyo	さまざま	sama zama
こねこね	kone kone	●さむざむ	samu zamu
ごぼごぼ	gobo gobo	●さめざめ	same zame
ごほんごほん	gohon gohon	さやさや	saya saya
こまごま	koma goma	さらさら	sara sara

ざらざら	zara zara	●じゃぶじゃぶ	jabu jabu
さわさわ	sawa sawa	じゃらじゃら	jara jara
ざわざわ	zawa zawa	しゃりしゃり	shari shari
さんさん	san san	じゃりじゃり	jari jari
さんざん	san zan	しゃんしゃん	shan shan
ざんざん	zan zan	じゃんじゃん	jan jan
		しゅうしゅう	shū shū
じいじい	jii jii	じゅうじゅう	jū jū
しおしお	shio shio	しゅるしゅる	shuru shuru
しかじか	shika jika	しゅんしゅん	shun shun
じきじき	jiki jiki	じょきじょき	joki joki
●しくしく	shiku shiku	しょぼしょぼ	shobo shobo
じくじく	jiku jiku	じょりじょり	jori jori
●しげしげ	shige shige	じょろじょろ	joro joro
しこしこ	shiko shiko	しらじら	shira jira
●しずしず	shizu shizu	しらずしらず	shirazu shirazu
しとしと	shito shito	●じりじり	jiri jiri
●じとじと	jito jito	●じろじろ	jiro jiro
しなしな	shina shina	しわしわ	shiwa shiwa
しばしば	shiba shiba	●じわじわ	jiwa jiwa
●しぶしぶ	shibu shibu	じわりじわり	jiwari jiwari
しましま	shima shima	しんしん	shin shin
●しみじみ	shimi jimi	じんじん	jin jin
しめしめ	shime shime		
じめじめ	jime jime	●すいすい	sui sui
●しゃあしゃあ	shā shā	すうすう	sū sū
じゃあじゃあ	jā jā	すかすか	suka suka
しゃかしゃか	shaka shaka	●ずかずか	zuka zuka
じゃかじゃか	jaka jaka	●ずきずき	zuki zuki
しゃきしゃき	shaki shaki	ずきんずきん	zukin zukin
しゃなりしゃなり	shanari shanari	●すくすく	suku suku

すけすけ	sukesuke	それぞれ	sorezore
●ずけずけ	zukezuke	●そろそろ	sorosoro
●すごすご	sugosugo	●ぞろぞろ	zorozoro
ずしんずしん	zushinzushin	そろりそろり	sororisorori
すたすた	sutasuta	●そわそわ	sowasowa
●ずたずた	zutazuta		
すっすっ	sussu(s)	たえだえ	taedae
すぱすぱ	supasupa	たかだか	takadaka
ずばずば	zubazuba	だくだく	dakudaku
ずぶずぶ	zubuzubu	●たじたじ	tajitaji
すべすべ	subesube	ただただ	tadatada
すみずみ	sumizumi	たびたび	tabitabi
●すやすや	suyasuya	●だぶだぶ	dabudabu
●すらすら	surasura	たまたま	tamatama
ずらずら	zurazura	●たらたら	taratara
するする	surusuru	●だらだら	daradara
●ずるずる	zuruzuru	たんたん	tantan
●すれすれ	suresure	だんだん	dandan
ずんずん	zunzun	ちかちか	chikachika
		●ちくちく	chikuchiku
せいせい	seisei	●ちびちび	chibichibi
ぜいぜい	zeizei	ちまちま	chimachima
ぜえぜえ	zēzē	ちゃかちゃか	chakachaka
●せかせか	sekaseka	ちゃきちゃき	chakichaki
せっせせっせ	sessesesse	ちゃくちゃく	chakuchaku
		ちゃぽちゃぽ	chapochapo
そうそう	sōsō	ちゃらちゃら	charachara
●ぞくぞく	zokuzoku	ちゅうちゅう	chūchū
そこそこ	sokosoko	ちゅんちゅん	chunchun
そもそも	somosomo	ちょいちょい	choichoi
そよそよ	soyosoyo		

ちょきちょき	choki choki	とうとう	tō tō
ちょくちょく	choku choku	どうどう	dō dō
●ちょこちょこ	choko choko	どかどか	doka doka
ちょぼちょぼ	chobo chobo	ときどき	toki doki
ちょろちょろ	choro choro	●どきどき	doki doki
ちょんちょん	chon chon	とくとく	toku toku
●ちらちら	chira chira	どくどく	doku doku
ちりちり	chiri chiri	とげとげ	toge toge
ちりんちりん	chirin chirin	とことこ	toko toko
ちろちろ	chiro chiro	どさどさ	dosa dosa
ちんちん	chin chin	どしどし	doshi doshi
		どすどす	dosu dosu
ついつい	tsui tsui	とつとつ	totsu totsu
つうつう	tsū tsū	とびとび	tobi tobi
●つかつか	tsuka tsuka	●とぼとぼ	tobo tobo
つぎつぎ	tsugi tsugi	どぼんどぼん	dobon dobon
つくづく	tsuku zuku	どやどや	doya doya
つねづね	tsune zune	どれどれ	dore dore
つぶつぶ	tsubu tsubu	とろとろ	toro toro
●つやつや	tsuya tsuya	●どろどろ	doro doro
つらつら	tsura tsura	●とんとん	ton ton
●つるつる	tsuru tsuru	●どんどん	don don
●つんつん	tsun tsun		
		●なあなあ	nā nā
てかてか	teka teka	なかなか	naka naka
でかでか	deka deka	●ながなが	naga naga
●てくてく	teku teku	なくなく	naku naku
でぶでぶ	debu debu	なみなみ	nami nami
てらてら	tera tera	●なよなよ	nayo nayo
●でれでれ	dere dere		
でんでん	den den	●にこにこ	niko niko

にじにじ	niji niji	●はきはき	haki haki
にたにた	nita nita	●ぱくぱく	paku paku
にちゃにちゃ	nicha nicha	ばさばさ	basa basa
にまにま	nima nima	ぱさぱさ	pasa pasa
にゃあにゃあ	nyā nyā	ばしばし	bashi bashi
●にやにや	niya niya	ばしゃばしゃ	basha basha
にゅるにゅる	nyuru nyuru	はたはた	hata hata
にょきにょき	nyoki nyoki	●ばたばた	bata bata
●にょろにょろ	nyoro nyoro	ぱたぱた	pata pata
		ぱちぱち	pachi pachi
●ぬくぬく	nuku nuku	ばちゃばちゃ	bacha bacha
ぬけぬけ	nuke nuke	はてはて	hate hate
ぬめぬめ	nume nume	はやばや	haya baya
ぬらぬら	nura nura	●はらはら	hara hara
●ぬるぬる	nuru nuru	●ばらばら	bara bara
		ぱらぱら	para para
●ねちねち	nechi nechi	●ばりばり	bari bari
ねとねと	neto neto	ぱりぱり	pari pari
●ねばねば	neba neba	はるばる	haru baru
		はればれ	hare bare
のうのう	nō nō	ばんばん	ban ban
●のこのこ	noko noko	ぱんぱん	pan pan
のしのし	noshi noshi		
●のそのそ	noso noso	ひいひい	hii hii
のっしのっし	nosshi nosshi	びいびい	bii bii
●のびのび	nobi nobi	ぴいぴい	pii pii
●のろのろ	noro noro	ひえびえ	hie bie
		●ぴかぴか	pika pika
はあはあ	hā hā	●ひくひく	hiku hiku
はいはい	hai hai	●びくびく	biku biku
ぱかぱか	paka paka	ぴくぴく	piku piku

ぴこぴこ	biko biko	●ひりひり	hiri hiri
ぴこぴこ	piko piko	●びりびり	biri biri
ひさびさ	hisa bisa	ぴりぴり	piri piri
ひしひし	hishi hishi	ひろびろ	hiro biro
びしびし	bishi bishi	ひんひん	hin hin
ぴしぴし	pishi pishi	びんびん	bin bin
●びしょびしょ	bisho bisho	ぴんぴん	pin pin
●ひそひそ	hiso hiso		
ひたひた	hita hita	ふうふう	fū fū
ぴたぴた	pita pita	ぶうぶう	bū bū
ぴちぴち	pichi pichi	ぷうぷう	pū pū
びちゃびちゃ	bicha bicha	ふかふか	fuka fuka
ぴちゃぴちゃ	picha picha	ふかぶか	fuka buka
びちょびちょ	bicho bicho	ぶかぶか	buka buka
●ひやひや	hiya hiya	ぷかぷか	puka puka
ひゃらひゃら	hyara hyara	●ぶくぶく	buku buku
ひゅうひゅう	hyū hyū	ぷくぷく	puku puku
びゅうびゅう	byū byū	ふさふさ	fusa fusa
ぴゅうぴゅう	pyū pyū	ぶすぶす	busu busu
ひゅるひゅる	hyuru hyuru	ふつふつ	futsu futsu
びゅんびゅん	byun byun	●ぶつぶつ	butsu butsu
ひょいひょい	hyoi hyoi	ぷつぷつ	putsu putsu
ひょうひょう	hyō hyō	ふにゃふにゃ	funya funya
ひょこひょこ	hyoko hyoko	ぶよぶよ	buyo buyo
ぴょこぴょこ	pyoko pyoko	ふらふら	fura fura
ぴよぴよ	piyo piyo	●ぶらぶら	bura bura
●ひょろひょろ	hyoro hyoro	ぶりぶり	buri buri
●ぴょんぴょん	pyon pyon	ぷりぷり	puri puri
●ひらひら	hira hira	ぷりんぷりん	purin purin
びらびら	bira bira	●ぶるぶる	buru buru
ぴらぴら	pira pira	ぶるんぶるん	burun burun

203

ふわふわ	fuwa fuwa	ぽいぽい	poi poi
ふんふん	fun fun	ほうぼう	hō bō
ぶんぶん	bun bun	ぼうぼう	bō bō
●ぷんぷん	pun pun	●ほかほか	hoka hoka
		●ぽかぽか	poka poka
へいへい	hei hei	ぼきぼき	boki boki
ぺいぺい	pei pei	ぽきぽき	poki poki
ぺかぺか	peka peka	ほくほく	hoku hoku
へこへこ	heko heko	ぼこぼこ	boko boko
べこべこ	beko beko	ぽこぽこ	poko poko
●ぺこぺこ	peko peko	●ぼさぼさ	bosa bosa
へたへた	heta heta	ぼそぼそ	boso boso
●べたべた	beta beta	ぼたぼた	bota bota
ぺたぺた	peta peta	●ぽたぽた	pota pota
べちゃべちゃ	becha becha	ぼちぼち	bochi bochi
ぺちゃぺちゃ	pecha pecha	ぽちぽち	pochi pochi
●へとへと	heto heto	ぼちゃぼちゃ	bocha bocha
べとべと	beto beto	ぽちゃぽちゃ	pocha pocha
ぺとぺと	peto peto	ぼつぼつ	botsu botsu
●へなへな	hena hena	ぽつぽつ	potsu potsu
●へらへら	hera hera	ぼつりぼつり	botsuri botsuri
●べらべら	bera bera	ぽつんぽつん	potsun potsun
●ぺらぺら	pera pera	ぼてぼて	bote bote
べりべり	beri beri	ほとほと	hoto hoto
へろへろ	hero hero	ほどほど	hodo hodo
べろべろ	bero bero	ぼとぼと	boto boto
●ぺろぺろ	pero pero	ぽとぽと	poto poto
べろんべろん	beron beron	ほのぼの	hono bono
ぺんぺん	pen pen	●ほやほや	hoya hoya
		ぼやぼや	boya boya
ほいほい	hoi hoi	ぼりぼり	bori bori

204

ぽりぽり	pori pori	みゃくみゃく	myaku myaku
ほれぼれ	hore bore	みりみり	miri miri
ほろほろ	horo horo	みるみる	miru miru
●ぼろぼろ	boro boro		
ぽろぽろ	poro poro	●むかむか	muka muka
ぼろんぼろん	boron boron	むくむく	muku muku
ぽろんぽろん	poron poron	むざむざ	muza muza
ぼんぼん	bon bon	●むしむし	mushi mushi
ぽんぽん	pon pon	むしゃむしゃ	musha musha
		●むずむず	muzu muzu
まあまあ	mā mā	むちむち	muchi muchi
まえまえ	mae mae	●むにゃむにゃ	munya munya
まごまご	mago mago	むらむら	mura mura
まざまざ	maza maza	●むんむん	mun mun
●まじまじ	maji maji		
ますます	masu masu	めいめい	mei mei
まずまず	mazu mazu	めえめえ	mē mē
またまた	mata mata	●めきめき	meki meki
●まだまだ	mada mada	●めそめそ	meso meso
●まちまち	machi machi	めためた	meta meta
まにまに	mani mani	めちゃめちゃ	mecha mecha
まるまる	maru maru	めらめら	mera mera
まんまん	man man	めりめり	meri meri
		めろめろ	mero mero
みいんみいん	miin miin	めんめん	men men
●みえみえ	mie mie		
みしみし	mishi mishi	もうもう	mō mō
みしりみしり	mishiri mishiri	もくもく	moku moku
みすみす	misu misu	もぐもぐ	mogu mogu
みちみち	michi michi	もこもこ	moko moko
みなみな	mina mina	もごもご	mogo mogo

もしもし	moshi moshi	よたよた	yota yota
●もじもじ	moji moji	よちよち	yochi yochi
もしゃもしゃ	mosha mosha	よなよな	yona yona
もじゃもじゃ	moja moja	●よぼよぼ	yobo yobo
もそもそ	moso moso	よりより	yori yori
もぞもぞ	mozo mozo	よれよれ	yore yore
●もたもた	mota mota	●よろよろ	yoro yoro
もてもて	mote mote		
もともと	moto moto	らくらく	raku raku
もやもや	moya moya	らんらん	ran ran
●もりもり	mori mori		
もろもろ	moro moro	りいんりいん	riin riin
●もんもん	mon mon	りゅうりゅう	ryū ryū
		りんりん	rin rin
やあやあ	yā yā		
やいやい	yai yai	るいるい	rui rui
やいのやいの	yaino yaino	るんるん	run run
●やすやす	yasu yasu		
やまやま	yama yama	れろれろ	rero rero
やみやみ	yami yami	れんれん	ren ren
やれやれ	yare yare		
		●ろうろう	rō rō
●ゆうゆう	yū yū	ろくろく	roku roku
ゆくゆく	yuku yuku		
●ゆさゆさ	yusa yusa	わあわあ	wā wā
ゆめゆめ	yume yume	●わいわい	wai wai
●ゆらゆら	yura yura	●わくわく	waku waku
●ゆるゆる	yuru yuru	わさわさ	wasa wasa
		●わざわざ	waza waza
よいよい	yoi yoi	わなわな	wana wana
よくよく	yoku yoku	●わんわん	wan wan
よしよし	yoshi yoshi		

このリストでは、「きゃっきゃっ」などつまる音で終わる語の場合、最後のアルファベットは仮表記であることを示すため（ ）で括った。実際には次に続く語の最初の子音で表される。

In the case of words in the foregoing list that end with the onset of a double consonant, such as *kyakkya(k)*, the final letter is placed in parentheses to indicate that it is tentative. In actual writing it is shown as the first consonant of the following word.

Example	きゃっきゃっ	kyakkya(k)
	↓	
	きゃっきゃっとさわぐ	kyakkyatto sawagu

本文辞書
作 成　大山直美
英 訳　ジョン・タラント
デザイン　SUPER TACO INC.
　　　　　小林　隆
　　　　　平塚雅人

英語人と日本語人のための
日本語擬態語辞典

1989年12月5日　　初版発行
1999年1月20日　　第14刷発行
著　者　五味太郎
　　　　©1989 by GOMI Taro
発行者　小笠原敏晶
発行所　株式会社ジャパンタイムズ
　　　　〒108-0023　東京都港区芝浦4丁目5番地4号
　　　　電話　(03)3453-2013(出版営業)
　　　　　　　(03)3453-2797(出版編集)
　　　　振替口座　00190-6-64848
印刷所　株式会社 太平印刷社

定価はカバーに表示してあります。
ISBN4-7890-0482-1